100 FRESH ALASKAN POEMS 2026

10 POETS 10 POEMS

ALEXIS GARCIA   "PRNSIS" BAYINNA BALLARD

KERSTEN CHRISTIANSON   RIDLEY JOLENA

REBECCA GOODRICH   ERIC GORDON JOHNSON

RAIF JOHNSON-KENNEDY   VIVIAN FAITH PRESCOTT

JULIE WHATMOUGH   ZOE WOODS

EDITED BY

M.C. MOHAGANI MAGNETEK

100 FRESH ALASKAN POEMS 2026

Dedicated to the marginalized, ignored and written-off poets.

We have a seat at the table because our words matter.

LAND & LABOR ACKNOWLEDGMENT

We acknowledge that our offices are located on the ancestral and unceded traditional territories of Indigenous Alaskan Natives. The Indigenous peoples of these lands and waters never surrendered lands or resources to Russia or the United States. We acknowledge this as both gratitude to the Indigenous communities who have held and continue to hold relationship with these lands and waters for generations and in recognition of the historical and ongoing legacy of colonialism. Additionally, we acknowledge this as a point of reflection for us all as we work towards actively dismantling colonial practices.

We recognize and acknowledge the labor upon which our country, state, and institution are built. We remember that our country was built on the labor of enslaved people who were kidnapped and brought to the US from the African continent and recognize the continued contribution of their survivors. We also acknowledge all immigrant and indigenous labor, including voluntary, involuntary, trafficked, forced, and undocumented peoples who contributed to the building of the country and continue to serve within our labor force. We recognize that our country is continuously defined, supported, and built upon by oppressed communities and peoples. We acknowledge labor inequities and the shared responsibility for combating oppressive systems in our daily work.

CONTENTS

THE MANY FRESH POETIC VOICES OF ALASKA: AN INTRODUCTION

"100 FRESH ALASKAN POEMS 2026" unites ten poets who capture Alaska's complexity and spirit. This anthology explores contemporary Alaskan realities—landscapes, challenges, and emotions—through varied voices. This essay examines the anthology's organization, core themes, stylistic range, and the environment's influence. In doing so, it shows why this collection is vital to understanding Alaskan literary identity and culture.

Organization and Editorial Vision

The anthology's structure is both thoughtful and deliberate. Each of the ten poets is given a dedicated section of ten poems, which opens with a biographical sketch and a synopsis of their poetic contribution. This approach does more than introduce the poets; it contextualizes their writing within their lived experiences, backgrounds, and personal histories. For readers—both those familiar with Alaskan poetry and those encountering it for the first time—these introductions lay the groundwork for empathy and understanding. The poets' biographies highlight involvement in writing groups, literary journals, engagement, and activism. The synopses also provide thematic signposts, allowing readers to anticipate the emotional terrain of each section before delving into the poems themselves; a literary uncommonness, considering many poetry books fail to offer the readers insight into the poets' intentions or some sort of interpretive guide for the readers to have an enhanced understanding of the poetics in question. Overall, the editorial vision is to foster inclusivity and narrative layering, intentionally bringing in voices that reflect Alaska's vast diversity beyond ongoing hegemonic perspectives. The anthology seeks to shift the literary landscape from one typically populated by well-educated, middle-aged writers with access to formal development to one that creates opportunities for those not hitherto represented. This includes marginalized writers such as high school poets, first-time poets, LGBTQ+ community members, and others who may lack formal credentials or have limited access to publishing. By doing so, the collection deliberately aims to expand and democratize Alaskan literary culture.

Identity, Survival, Transformation, and Alaska as Character

One of the anthology's strengths is the intentional inclusion of poets from diverse backgrounds, ages, and identities. The collection features Alexis Garcia's journey of bicultural identity and language acquisition. It also highlights Ridley Jolena's candid narration of survival through violence. The poets reveal both vulnerability and complexity. This diversity is not performative. It is central to the anthology's ethos and creates a chorus that is both rich and discordant, echoing Alaska's diversity. The anthology features poets who identify as queer, Indigenous, immigrants, veterans, and survivors. It avoids offering a single portrait of Alaska. Instead, it insists on multiplicity and the value of each poet's truth. Alaska's natural world is central to the discussion. The landscape is omnipresent in these poems. It serves as a setting, a participant, an adversary, and a source of solace. Kersten Christianson's Yukon wanderings, Zoe Woods' wilderness explorations, and Vivian Faith Prescott's depictions of anxiety draw on the land's physicality and symbolism. Animals such as bears, moose, and wolves are frequently depicted. Motifs like the moon, wind, and tides are also common. These elements show the interconnectedness of human and non-human life. Nature mirrors internal states, acts as a catalyst for transformation, and can be a force to endure. The poets' varying relationships with the environment prompt questions about belonging, stewardship, and the cost of resilience in a beautiful but dangerous world.

One of the anthology's most striking features is its thematic multiplicity and depth. The poets each bring unique voices, but several recurring motifs connect their work. These include identity, survival, transformation, and the state of Alaska as a character. The themes are explored in turn, offering insights into experiences across the anthology. For example, Alexis Garcia's poems use the moon as a recurring metaphor for bicultural identity, displacement, and aspiration. Julie Whatmough's section addresses sexual trauma and the reclamation of womanhood. Her writing is both an act of personal healing and a call for collective empowerment. She urges women to speak their truths and rewrite their stories.

Transformation is often catalyzed by Alaska's wild landscapes. Vivian Faith Prescott's "One Foot in the Wilderness" uses the natural world as both a metaphor and a medium for healing and change. Zoe Woods's writing is filled with textures and sounds of the wild—tidepools, glaciers, Sitka spruce, and midnight sun. Nature is sometimes a comfort, sometimes a cause for fear. Above all, it is a teacher. Rebecca Goodrich's poems, inspired by experiences in Unalaska, use wind and weather as metaphors for time, memory, and hope. Eric Gordon Johnson's work examines animal mortality, predation, and ethical questions that stem from human interaction with nature. Whether describing bears or changing seasons, the poets always return to the idea of adaptation. Both people and animals must change to survive.

Stylistic Diversity and Innovation

The anthology stands out for its stylistic breadth. Poetic forms range from traditional haibun and free verse to confessional, narrative, and experimental poetry. This miscellany reflects the collection's themes. It lets poets use various modes of storytelling and expression. For example, Christianson's haibun blends prose with haiku, creating a rhythm like the pulse of the land. Woods's work adopts a diaristic tone. Whatmough combines lyric intensity with direct address, inviting readers into deeply emotional spaces. "PRNsis" Bayinna Ballard's collection of poems uses vernacular language and social media motifs. These interrogate identity, self-worth, and community. Raif Johnson-Kennedy offers stream-of-consciousness free-verse, lore, and spoken-word stylistics. This expands the anthology's motivation of encouragement and perseverance.

Community is a recurring theme in the anthology. It is seen both as a support system and as an audience. Many poets are involved in local literary groups, activist circles, and family networks. Their writing is shaped by these connections. Choosing to share deeply personal stories, especially about trauma and marginalization, raises ethical questions about representation. Who gets to tell which stories? How can poets honor their truth without silencing others? The anthology models ethical storytelling based on listening, humility, and openness to dialogue. In doing so, it challenges readers and writers to consider their responsibilities within literary and social communities. The anthology also prompts discussion about the future of Alaskan poetry. In a rapidly changing world—culturally, environmentally, and technologically—how will Alaskan poets define themselves and their work? Including voices such as Johnson-Kennedy and Garcia demonstrates the editors' commitment to renewal and innovation. This is why 'Fresh' appears in the anthology's title. At the same time, the anthology's engagement with environmental changes, cultural memory, and community resilience suggests that the poets' work will remain vital as both art and advocacy. Publishing these poems may reach readers who relate to the experiences explored in the anthology.

Conclusion

"100 Fresh Alaskan Poems 2026" is more than just a collection of poems—it makes a clear statement. The book shows that Alaskan literature belongs to everyone shaped by this difficult land, not just those with formal writing credentials or literary status. By including poets with experiences ranging from foster care to academia, immigration to Indigenous identity, and queerness to survival, the anthology challenges old ideas about who is considered a poet. Through a structured, varied approach and meaningful themes, the book brings together many voices that do not always agree and does not try to force a single answer.

Alaska here is both beautiful and brutal, nurturing and indifferent—a landscape that demands honesty. The poets answer that demand with courage. They write not from a safe distance, but from the full weight of their experience. Trauma is not made into art; it is recognized. Nature is not idealized; it is faced. Most importantly, this anthology insists on poetry's social role. These poems are not just for admiration. They are for connection, healing, and resistance. In Jolena's survival stories, Whatmough's reclamation of womanhood, Garcia's search for belonging, and Johnson-Kennedy's urgency, poetry becomes testimony. The anthology shows a literary community built not on exclusion, but on the radical act of listening. As Alaska changes—its glaciers receding, its communities evolving, its cultural identity challenged—collections like this will serve as vital records. They show not only what this place looks like, but what it feels like to live, struggle, and find meaning here. "100 Fresh Alaskan Poems 2026" marks a pivotal moment. It suggests a more inclusive, honest, and vital future for Alaskan poetic voices.

-M.C. MoHagani Magnetek, Editor

PART ONE
MY SOUL BECAME THE MOON

ALEXIS GARCIA

ABOUT THE POET: ALEXIS GARCIA

ALEXIS GARCIA LIVES IN ANCHORAGE, Alaska, but was raised in the Dominican Republic. He moved to Alaska at age 11, where he started living with his grandparents. Now a junior at East High School, he recalls arriving in Alaska speaking only his native language; within two months, English became his primary language, though he still uses his native tongue. In his freshman year, his passion for writing began after noticing that most movies do not represent his people or, when they do, rely on hurtful stereotypes. He began writing, found a connection to all his work, and felt his writing served as a diary. His short-term goal is to write a novel and, with his grandparents' permission, publish it. He hopes to be an amazing director in the future, with dream studios including A24 and Marvel Studios. Growing up with Marvel comics and discovering their movies inspired him to write scripts he hopes to send as an adult. His long-term goals include winning at least two Oscars, becoming known worldwide, and ensuring people see themselves in his movies. He wants to inspire other teens to pursue their dreams, no matter the obstacles.

SYNOPSIS

MY SOUL BECAME THE MOON

My Soul Became the Moon is a series of poems reflecting on my life and personality, using the moon as an allusion. The moon is a beautiful symbol with its own stories; by drawing on them, it can become a powerful metaphor.

THE MOON YOUR EYES

The moon, your eyes, the sky, your lens
Seeing the message from the stars
For something's beyond,
Acting like nothing's behind

Looking back is the shadow that lurks
The abyss of secrets and lies
Hissing your name.
"Stay back," they say

Forward the stars and the cosmos
Backward the past leeches
Tempted to look back
Knowing to keep forward

The past that person left in the mirror
The future, a nebula by your side
All the planets aligned for greatness

The moon, your eyes, the sky, your lens
Seeing the message from the stars
See is beyond like nothing behind

BLOOD MOON

Once bright silver like a pearl
Now stained with the anger
She tried vigorously to suppress.

Once, she was admired for her delicate beauty
Now, feared for her unfulfilled rage
She was a symbol of elegance,
Self-control and courage
Acting with vengeance in her face.

Monitoring the skies with her red light
Looking for the ones that wronged her
The tears that ran down her face
Replaced by the blood of her foes.

Her enemies feel her bleak stare
While she invariably follows
Her once star-like eyes
Now covered with wrath.

ASK AND YOU SHALL RECEIVE

My knees in the ground I beg,
Begging for your guiding light
Illuminate my path to greatness.

My hands high reaching you,
Praying for the silver of your skin
Turns many years into my success.

My eyes cry rivers of gold,
The gold I seem to have
The gold that will come along the way.

My soul reflects your beauty,
The stars and the cosmos.
One day when I die
My soul will merge with yours,

Your light shines in my eyes,
Making the gold gleam
With your presence, the answer I seek
Who will become my dream.

MOONQUAKES

If the moon quakes
No one is there to feel it
Was she harmed?

Skin reflects the blissful sun
Body moves the tides with its curves
Eyes watchfully watching us

Many see your beautiful side
They stare with awe.
When your body breaks
The cracks hidden by the shadow you cast
People oblivious of the scars

Alone you deal with pain
Around people you fake a smile
You scream to the stars your hardship
But they neglect your cry for help

When the moon quakes
Even if there is no one to feel it
The cracks in her divine body
Are evidence of the damage.

NOTHING BUT A BLACK MOON

A void all around me
No star to guide my way
Just a flame that taunts me

When I get closer she is further
I never seem to catch her
Sometimes I get close
But the flame laughs and goes her way

I've stopped trying and each time
The flame's laughter and light
Faints slowly

Without her now I understand
She was my star
That guide that I plead for

No way of getting her back
All I'm left with is nothing
But a black moon

WHY SO BLUE?

Dearest Moon, why gloomy?
You're silver, like a fox in winter
Now turned into a poisonous glaucus.

My beloved, your sadness reflects in your soul
across all oceans.
It wraps the earth like winter.

Your body now colored by grief
And its awful palettes
Around you, a cloudy storm
Waiting for your command to strike.

Is it worth being blue for your sorrows?
I'll take and bury them
In my stone cold heart.

I will bring you your light
And wrap it in a bow.
I don't like seeing you like this
Even if it's once a blue moon.

I SEE YOU

Dressed in your silver dress
While crying in the sky
Your makeup from the cosmos
Running down your divine face

Feeling like no one sees you
You dim the light
That made you bright

What you don't know
Someone down from earth
Recognized how you change
From black to grey
And crescent to full

When you're once blue
He sees it too
When your anger fills you red
He watches with awe

Thinking no one sees you
Dressed in your silver dress
I see you for what you are
Once blue filled with red
I see you when you go
From black to grey
Crescent to full

WEREWOLF BY SHADE

In the day, your words bubbly
Joyful, and cloud smooth.
I take them with the warmth
In the sly tone meant for them.

For others the light you bring
Is brighter than the rays of the sun.
They believe your sweet words,
Eating them like a candy house.

As the sun goes West for its rest
The moon takes its celestial place
And that's when everything changed.

Your wool fur sheds
Revealing your sharp claws,
Once innocent eyes turn predator.
Now every word,
A bite you take out of my flesh.
The dark and the shadow are your home
For you to show your big wolf ears.

In the day a sweet lamb,
The misty moon comes
And you transform.

THE MOON CONTROLS THE TIDES, BUT I CAN'T CONTROL YOU

Her majestic light guiding the waves,
Her perfect shape reflected in the ocean.
She pulls the tides with her magic
Moving the ocean with just a glance.

I wish to be her, my so big you
Can't help but be close.
My magic can only get me so far.
Friends, and strangers pulled,
The only one my gravity cannot get is you.

I'm not like the moon,
She controls waves and tides.
The ocean can't help but obey her.

I'm mere dust in her tornado,
An after sound of her earthquake.
I'm there, but the moon shines brighter
Each day, getting your attention.

WHERE I KEEP YOU
I KEEP THE MOON

My body a vessel my mind a disciple
My heart is where I have kept you
You will have company of the pearl

Your lips the black hole I'm sucked in
The stars sing your name in a choir
My soul dances to the melody

My eyes see the nebula in you
A sun they do not want to look away from
Like a moth in search of light

In my heart I keep you
my spirit dwells with yours
In there is the moon
Right beside the heart-shaped door

The moon with her silver skin
Compelled to you hides in my heart too
The two of you shining so bright
Filling me with bliss

SOMETHING TO DO WITH THE WIND

REBECCA GOODRICH

ABOUT THE POET: REBECCA GOODRICH

IN 1994, Rebecca Goodrich left the fool's gold of California to build a houseboat in Unalaska. Within a few days, future Alaska writer laureate, Jerah Chadwick, took her under his wing and helped her enroll, as a directed study student, for college classes on the island. This was one of many dreams that Alaska has returned and revealed to Goodrich since then. She hopes to return the many favors by keeping Alaska alive, in both word and deed. Rebecca Goodrich, consulting editor and author, lives in Anchorage, an active member of the Alaskan literary community.

SYNOPSIS

SOMETHING TO DO
WITH THE WIND

My life in poetry and writing has meant hundreds of pieces, from haiku to memoir. This set of ten poems on one thread required strenuous assembling of poems, as if they were found in a shattered mosaic in an archeological dig, to find the steps of truths and their order, despite any chronology. As with much art, our human timekeeping is useless. Yes, poetry can foretell the future. Yes, poetry can redefine and illuminate the past. Yet both of these uses for poetry will, at times, fail us. We are only human. Perhaps this is why so much of my poetry attaches itself to that which is, if not eternal, then much more durable than my blood and tears.

SOMETHING TO DO WITH THE WIND

here at the edge of the world
we all have something to do with the wind
when it blows
some of us stay safe indoors
and some walk naked into the storm
oh, must be something to do with the wind
must be something to do with the wind

we live all the time with the wind
it's the air we breathe
it's the clouds we climb
it's always on the move
no matter what the time

it carries the words between us
some of us have nothing to say
and some have nothing to lose
oh, must be something to do with the wind
must be something to do with the wind

we live every day with the wind
sometimes it does us harm
it shakes our foundations
and tears us apart
it scatters our love
and blows away our hearts
no matter how strong we are at the start

must be something to do with the wind

oh, must be something to do with the wind

[Unalaska Island, 1997]

1967

I fell in love
with this cool green earth
once when
a long age ago
sky was blue
and grass was green
and both were frosted with gold

Hand in hand we walked
my lover and me
upon the hills of earth
Then I forsook my lover's hand
and took the hand of earth

[1967]

THE TERRACED LAND, PALOS VERDES

Breaking and reforming
the land is one story
over and over again
the theme one of glory

For through erosion and unfolding
though it rills like waves
or sharps with cataclysmic shakes
the story remains unbroken
The ground can become upbraided
yet done again become the same

From cliff on shore to sand
to rock again
Understand then
the minerals deepen
from quartz to apatite
The sun bakes the ground
the waters
always coming
release it
to make mud to make rock
to catch fossils in their falling
from fact to contemplation

Think apace
pace slowly

The terraced land
no Inca created

no farmer filled or cleared stones away
This island
sectioned like shale
making of these high hills
a series of resting places

[1971]

CABRILLO BEACH SUNSET

from the city to San Pedro we drove
with our thoughts following us
like the leaves that clattered
at our feet on the windy street
walking down to the shore

and here we are
the clouds layered step by step
advance and retreat

arranged across the edge of tide
the surfers dressed like seals wait
to meet the waves

some are lifted high
some still wait

and oh the sky is pink and blue
in sections and then gray
and then black
but with a glow that keeps
the heart and eyes carried high
and soaring
throughout the night

[1978]

1968

Harboring, like the current
past Portuguese Bend
where the water rushes skeptically,
the continent ends
dividing California among the tides.

We all are ships in this night
passing portal after port
the wind cries at the ocean's side
and phosphorescent fishes
turn and twist in our minds,
lighting the firmament below the sky.

What remains to those who abide
when thoughts are sent forth,
into this night,
and come not, not once more homeward?
The echo she returns alone.

The oceans billow green and gray
along the harsh coastal ways of life.
I will not let the tide steal me away;
even solitary, even lonely,
I hear the sound. I know the story.

[1968]

HAVE YOU NOT ADMIRED HOUNDS

Have you not admired pink-tinted hounds
chained about the throat
with colored links
to match their manicures;
so trained to the leash they know the rhinestoned length
and how far they may prance
before the strain shows?

It is the wild things
who in pursuit of their fate,
when set upon by traps
have been known to break
through their very bones.
By their own pain they make their path known—
to live free
if even on three legs they go.

[1974]

FALLING

First time I'd ever seen
icicles in April, having been
too long in the south.
In the Bering Sea
it was winter, snow to my knees,
grasping even my hips
freezing bones still in shock
from the emptiness and silence
of the gray Aleutian sky.

Out on the hills we walked that day,
my lover and I, the afternoon longer
than what seemed natural
to the softer-latitudes bred.
He bounding ahead,
I blindly laboring behind,
falling now and then
into hidden rivulets, grazing
torn walls of Quonset huts, where
jeeps parked long ago
in the war my father fought.

Chris threw himself down
To rest, I thought,
but I pushed forward
still blindly, still blind.
One more tired step, then I stalled
not even seeing the edge,
white on white
the thousand feet down.

One half step more

and the air, its mercy porous
would have given
my bones and blood
to the rocks beneath its flowing currents.
I would have been washed away.
What could have been left
is all that has remained
--my feathered heart--
riding the winds
Of that lost, wild place

    [2000]

Abridged version edited by poet Anne Coray for Invocations anthology, which did not come to fruition.

FLIGHT HOME TO UNALASKA

Will I make it home? It's a question we ask
when we climb into the airplane
take off our hats, stuff gloves into pockets,
slip off our boots. We relax. Take-off is always
fine. We wiggle our toes inside our socks
and head off for the bush.

As many variegated edges as a river,
has this frontier of ours.
Some have names: Dillingham, King Cove, False Pass.
Farther west, we slip into vowels and soft aspirates: Unga,
Belkofski, Ounalashka.
The syllables soften, like the endless clouds
the engines are pushing through,
an altitude eternal, infinitely blue.

The sound creeps into our heads.
The pros wear earplugs or speak
loudly, already deaf.
Yawn, cat-nap, or hash over old times,
next year's fish and caribou.

It's a hunting trip now;
we are tracking down land.
It's out there somehow,
floating in this mist-wrapped world
floating otherworldly, out of reach.
We will never touch down.
We have been flying for hours now.

You never step onto the same island twice.
Yet it is home, there it is!
We find it bobbing on the waves
near its customary location
athwart two great, unruly oceans
whose friction creates the air we use
to touch down.

We bid the mountains stand back,
give us passage to the air strip.
We approach the field—a flat place—

arm-wrestled from land that was rocky
for millions of years.
We hold our breath,
to show the wind how to do the same;
each landing a cooperative effort, much like
fishing, fighting, loving.

We feel the wheels bounce down
the thrusters blast to restrain the jet
before its nose gets wet in Dutch Harbor.
Now we exhale, now we applaud
how easy now
to believe in God,
the pilot, the mountains, the wind,
ourselves,
all the forces of nature
who have given us this day.

So many departures in Alaska life
so many turnarounds. So many hours of waiting
await us in Cold Bay.
Even the storms do not stay
forever, even they fly away
like the ravens

who greet us with the neighborhood news.

From their opened beaks
we hear the sound
oh we never understand.
All we know is touching down
and walking upon the land.

[1997]

Previously published: Alaska Women Speak, Fall 1998; Between Two
Rivers anthology, 2000. All rights retained by author. Broadside with
author's photography at Great Harvest Bakery exhibition, Anchorage,
Alaska.

MOTHER PLATONIDA GROMOFF 1928-1997

WHO DIED AT
HOME IN UNALASKA

Sometimes things are thrust upon you
into your hands and you hold them
as long as you can and then
the williwaw blows down from the mountains
and loosens your grip
you just let go
to seek the finer things—
cloud vapor, volcano smoke
long white feathers
from angel wings

I heard all your voices
all your words
but I let go of the talking
the reaching hands
let me go

The speaking halted
and I went into
the silence between the sea-waves
of the Bering.

[1997]

Text aired as a PSA on Unalaska public TV station, KUCB, September
11, 1997 and perhaps for some days after. Rights retained by author.

OUR WORLD IS BUILT FROM MEMORY

our world is built from memory
and the appearance of all this
is starlight—removed from its source
possibly already passed from growth to non-existence

time is the root of all this earth
yet only the faithless call it false
blind their eyes
and deny all that ever happened

finding conjunction of what is
with what is not
is stumbling upon
some of the agony of the tongueless ocean
which, knowing all, cannot speak,
yet sometimes makes a joyful noise

for to stand inside oneself
and to sight also from the thin horizon line
is to understand the winds that have become
the shadows of your face
and to measure without touching
the joy at finding land

[1976]

Previously published: Golden Horses anthology, 1976. Rights retained by author.

YUKON WANDERINGS

KERSTEN CHRISTIANSON

ABOUT THE POET: KERSTEN CHRISTIANSON

KERSTEN CHRISTIANSON DERIVES inspiration from wild, wanderings, and road trips. She has authored *The Ordering of Stars* (Sheila-Na-Gig, 2025), *Curating the House of Nostalgia* (Sheila-Na-Gig, 2020), *What Caught Raven's Eye* (Petroglyph Press, 2018), *and Something Yet to Be Named* (Kelsay Books, 2017). Additionally, she is the poetry editor of the quarterly journal, *Alaska Women Speak*. Kersten lives in Sitka, Alaska where she keeps an eye on the tides, shops Old Harbor Books, and hoards smooth ink pens.

SYNOPSIS

YUKON WANDERINGS

Yukon Wanderings is a gathering of poems born of nearly three decades exploring Yukon's vast and shifting landscapes – through the radiant sweep of summer light and the deep stillness of winter. Written largely in or about the North, these pieces return to themes of tending beneath endless skies, encounters with bears, the ache of loss, the unearthing of what was once hidden or forgotten – whether a mummified creature or a memory. Many take the shape of haibun, or partial haibun, a form that naturally unfolds amid Yukon's long days and far-reaching light. Others move freely through the cadence of verse, capturing moments of movement, solitude, and renewal. Threaded throughout is a reverence for wildness and the enduring freedom in moving forward, one landscape, one moment, one poem at a time.

PONDERING BLUE AT THE MILE 1016 PUB IN THE JUNCTION

"Pompeii Excavation Unveils Rare 'Blue Room' Believed to Be an Ancient Shrine." -Leah Sarnoff, ABC News

I have a fixation
on old things: wolf
pups, baby wooly
mammoths, and rooms
in blue scrawled
with seasons.

Just last weekend,
I placed a string
of wooden trade beads
Bruce found on the tundra
near Shaktoolik
in the hands of friends

who also marveled
at the things we can't
put a date on. Today,
I considered blue
as I discarded the gray,
woolen sweater

of coastal precipitation
for the tranquility
of robin's egg sky,
not so unlike the blue

pine floor at home,
both distressed, bright.

I could tattoo upon both
floor and sky words
of Fortymile gold dust,
Yukon cavorting, and love
along a muddy river:
roiling, swift.

Wolf pups and mammoths;
earth and sky; ink of Himalayan
poppies, blueberries flow
from the poet's needle.
Blue is a holy place,
a gathering of words.

EVOLUTION OF CAMPING

It's been days since I've brushed my hair. There are birds nesting in its tangled threads. Tim Hortons is still the best cheap coffee around. But what I'm really here to say is your girl still has it goin' on. I have graduated from former Tent Pole Holder to Tent Pitcher. It took a hot minute. Tight fly anchored, followed by some crystals and twinkle lights to make the behemoth shelter just a little more woo-woo. Tents hold wild magic, even after packed away for years. This one carries the scent of my family, our dogs in various phases of drying after a swim, bug dope, campfires, and every kilometer ticked off on some road trip, or another. The wrinkled fly suggests it was last packed away damp. There is tree-needled debris littering the floor. The windows zipped open to their last preferred setting. I've missed, without knowing to miss, the shadows of insects marching across the taut dome, branches playing shadow puppets in the lowering sun against stretched canvas. My hands were awkward in this set-up until muscle-memory kicked in. Many colorful words used in the process; a litany not worth repeating. Tonight, the wild roses bloom sweet, and I'm lucky in many things.

BEDAZZLING

Solstice lands like new footwear —
rugged Birkenstocks in Elemental Blue —
because if sky is too shy to flash its azure,
you still can savor how earth cradles
the foot that ventures forth to travel trail,

cross stream, amble the rainbow crosswalk
intersecting Main Street in downtown
Whitehorse. A passerby in this urban
boreal, your neck stretches in permeating
sun to look through shop windows for bits

and baubles: Raven mug by the artist
Hell Wench, new ceramic stink pot
for all the essential citrus oils to infuse
and steam with lavender and poems,
a short stack of poetry by Canadians,

because when in Canada…and best of all,
earrings from Adäka, caribou tracks
of shimmering beryl sky, milky gilded
florals, sauntering a high-circling sun path.
Beaded on smoked moose hide, they spin

and tangle in your unruly hair, the scent
of campfire and wind carried in the nape
of your neck. Swish of skirt, 30 days
ahead allow you to repeat this walk,
this route; don't squander the time.

IMPERMANENCE IS THE NATURE OF ALL THINGS

The afternoon shines like a new penny; the road to Skagway, an eye-catching heads-up. Your daughter mailed you a package from home and when you arrive to the front of the line at the always-hopping post office, the post mistress says for everyone to hear, *Christ, still with the General Delivery? Get a post office box already!* She remembers you from six years prior, writing poetry in a cabin at the end of many roads. You remember drinking gin with her on the distillery's porch in Haines. When you gather your goods from home (disco twinkle lights, med refill, tiny shells, bits of beach glass), you tell her, *See you in another six years, friend!* From there, a stop at Jeff's bookstore to pick up new poetry from X'unei Lance Twitchell and Linda Buckley. At the pink gas station where you once heard a cruise ship bellowing "It's a Wonderful World," bouncing off mountains, the guy filling your tank with unleaded loves your turquoise and goldenrod earrings. So does Sarah, waiting in line with you for your pad Thai orders from the Starfire food truck. Fat Buddha sits between two blooms stretching their vitamin orange, their violet jam, for daylight through the cracks of the logging cable spool table, Fat Buddha with gleaming copper coins as tiny offerings at his toes. Back home, the summer's losses are immeasurable; your community's collective pain travels the channels of the Inside Passage clear up to the boreal and beyond. Fat Buddha would probably remind you there's never really an end, but a continuum, but maybe that's not good enough. Sometimes that woo-woo, that pluck, that mad energy is your only move, the reach and ponder of a found penny, heads or tails, lifted from the shrapnel-littered path.

Tutshi Lake picnic:
Noodles, wind, playing catch up
with my one-time husband.

GRACE FOR THE URSUS ARCTOS HORRIBILIS

may the forest
sheltering any number
of human malfeasance

shuffle gentle breeze
against your upturned face
may you stretch your limbs

in the wind, invite warm sun
to caress your shoulders as you
change direction to exit a door

that was never yours to open   may
you recognize with open heart, clear
conscience, this lush dwelling

of birch, black spruce, of ursine
wandering their hallways, teaching
their young the sweetness of their world:

dandelion greens, berries and roots,
salmon's crimson flesh   may
you offer them wide berth

UNDER THE SECRETS ACT ONCE ILLUMINATED BY PERIMETER LIGHTS

"This building had big ears." -June Gaffin, The Yukoner Magazine #17

Up on Lobird perches the Radar Apartments, the moon-silver DEW-line station from an era of Cold War and espionage, divided now by paper-mâchéd walls, segmented into low-cost apartments. Birthed of metal, steel, 10-foot ceilings with wide-eyed windows historically shuttered, silent, locked. The Canadian Air Force once listened from here to the airwaves for Russian chatter and to report back to American military. Communication specialists called it the Squirrel Cage; civilians, the Listening Post. I call it Borrowed Home under the sun that spins tight circles like a child's toy top without ever tumbling. Between Yukon wild coffee brew in the morning, lemon lavender radler in the evening, the days' routine rolls out easily: Write the poems, listen to the wind, read the books, listen to the wind, again. Spooning this vortex, I dream with ears wide open, invite story to wash over me like moonlight. Here, I catch detritus of story passed along through the chatter of Paper Birch leaves: Old Crow woman overlooked in a winter ditch by RCMP who confused her for a discarded garbage bag; a son peddling pills, wearing vodka like a dousing of cologne. Back home, a young man walks his gentle heart into the woods, leaving us all devastated, hopeless. Where is the balance between ruin and euphoria?

Cut the chain link fence,
the barbed wire, to reveal
the poppy red raw.

CURIOSITY PIQUED

When you come across a single moose leg at the intersection and wonder the walking whereabouts of the remaining three; this could be a constellation, or a parable. That you listen to old country and the weekly Indigenous music chart toppers. That you spend an evening watching robin chase squirrel from nest, down trunk, through the July underbrush of absinthe and fresh celery green. When you take time to smell the wild Yukon roses in their throat-opening bloom, a Dairy Queen Blizzard in your hand. That lilacs and fireweed blooming simultaneously can alter the taste of honey. That a wasp is not a bee, the evidence of that, the stinger in your thumb. Even this, a blessing.

AND WHEN WE
TALK ABOUT BEARS

And there they traipse: sow,
her two cubs; their henna hides
ripple as their thick

bodies carve a wake
through verdant sedge of ocean-
side estuary. Bright

dahlias, russet bloom,
brown bears ebb and flow like tide
their short bloom sustained

by mixed greens and soon-berries;
to later feast on red-fleshed
salmon. For now, cubs standing

on short, rear legs. Mouths chock-full
of what sustains. Small faces upturned,
their short season warmed by evening sun.

FALL DOWN EIGHT TIMES; GET UP NINE, OR, TIME WELL-SPENT

Tuesday, and it's Wing Night at the Kopper King Neighbours Pub on the outskirts of Whitehorse. $9.15 a pound, eat-in only. I give this menu a sidelong look, once believed the place had to have been a magnificent steakhouse we never stopped at for one reason or another, only to learn its depth is quite shallow: Wings, domestic bottle beer, low-light dingy. I spent the whole of Monday in the lantern glow of the Old Snow Carver and his longtime Yukon stories. He once sold me a Raven Lady sculpture in full crouch, shoulders stout enough to carry the world, to carry my man from this lifetime to another. Like a farfetched Greek origin tale, Survival birthed from Absence and this Raven Lady took up residence on my desk as only a muse can. As we sipped cranberry and lavender raddlers from Yukon Brewing, he spouted stories of ice carving competitions in Quebec and Japan, of reading the weather for CBC and our common joy for words like *graupel*, how his first wife left him with two babies to raise, how it's possible to recover from most kinds of slip. We exhaled over shared insight of creative process while his hands shaped and molded a new Raven Lady for me.

When he asked me what characteristics she should have, I first tried to shrug off the inquiry as I'm introverted-inclined, but forged into what I secretly hoped would emerge: Big-breasted, on her knees provocative, head tilted, fiery hope and flirt and humor in her eyes. There is glazing and firing yet to do. Will she carry shades of shadow plum or Poseidon teal? How the arms take to flame will determine her outcome. I may not remember that Tuesday is Wing Night at Kopper King, and I don't really care about that, but I'll never forget how Donald Watt's hands forged flight from a block of clay in a Monday cabin.

> *Raven Lady guards my desk*
> *like a shiny thing;*
> *a lucky penny bauble.*

REVIVED BY FANG & CLAW

The North Klondike Highway runs 330 miles from Whitehorse to Dawson City. The road braids its way through the boreal to meet, greet, and at times, offer tender, temporary goodbye to the Yukon River, before reuniting again with an open-mouthed kiss upon your arrival. You can't travel this artery without a finger on the pulse of memory. You remember his lazy, left-handed, two-fingered steer, windows open, his lower lip packed with Copenhagen Snuff, his right hand on your thigh, your hair blowing in the wind like a Bob Dylan song. Eyes wild, kindled by cuss and spark, loonies and toonies clanking in the console, not jazz, but Tragically Hip cranked on the stereo: radio / cassette / CD / streamed. This time, you trip this road like a missile, brake hard to watch Braeburn elk, iPhone photo-shoot a grizzly bear clawing through packed dirt and root for sun-worshipping ground squirrels. Even a deer catches your eye, and you marvel at this unscreened wild; no filter. Not even the acreage of still-smoking wildfire can slow you down. You have a 3:30 appointment with Double Denim Tattoo; Bee is ready to ink Zhùr, a 57,000-year-old wolf pup on the arm of your writing hand. A 57,000-year-old-wolf pup who still has stories to tell: That her last meal was salmon, that she was crushed in her den, that she still travels north from a museum display to attend Tr'ondëk Hwëch'in First Nations gatherings, like Moosehide.

That she was found by miners in a goldfield outside of Dawson City. That she first appeared in a poem of yours in 2016, a haibun quite like this. And later, your finger traces this new art resting on a bed of flaming fireweed in your skin, you close your eyes and imagine the unruly nature of her copper pelt, that baby-soft animal fur of her. And later, you check into the magenta-trimmed Bunkhouse, walk the muddy, pot-holed street to the Back Alley Pizza Window. There, the old owner says to you in a thick, Italian accent, *Where is your man and your daughter?* as if no time had passed, as if seven years had not passed.

> To answer, I grasp
> at straws, the story too sad
> for such fine pizza.

A HUMAN CONDITION

RIDLEY JOLENA

ABOUT THE POET: RIDLEY JOLENA

I USE poetry as a way to survive in an increasingly unsurvivable world starting when I was born. I went through multiple foster homes, a seriously screwed-up group home, & seriously screwed-up adults that I am trying not to become. I'm a survivor of domestic violence as well as a survivor of rape by two people I dated & one person that I didn't know that drugged me. I also have survived multiple physical & sexual assaults as an adult & severe physical & emotional abuse as a child. Without writing I would have ended my life decades ago, that being said I am also a suicide survivor I am also now physically disabled & deal with debilitating nerve pain & cluster migraines. So in these ways, I'm blessed in understanding humanity in a way that a lot of people don't get to experience except maybe other writers. I mean why else does someone feel compelled to write poetry?

SYNOPSIS
A HUMAN CONDITION

I use poetry as a way to survive in an increasingly unsurvivable world.

WE DRIVE PAST THE POOR

We drive past the poor
Old lady aged more by poverty
Than the years marching across her sad face
Poor, A name that the labeling theory proves right
we treat people who have less
Call them unbecoming things
We hope never to be
When we shouldn't label
Them at all
Instead, we treat them
Like they have a Leprosy-like disease
When the have-nots
are not the ones clinically insane
I am guilty myself
We call the haves, rich
When in reality
They are heartless thieves
And yet the world turns
While people's heads are bent downward
scrolling on their phones
Glimpses of other rich people's lives
That don't have to deal
With the daily grind of just trying
To understand a not-very-understanding world.

TIME EVEN IF IT DOESN'T

Time even if it doesn't exist
Still changes you
 gives it
The objective reality
That we take for granted.
Why are we here?
Where are we going?
Where have we been?
And what was it all for?
Are we living for another?
Are we existing in a plane of denial?
Why do we care so much
When so many care so little?
I want to be able to hide my heart
Unroll my sleeve
Keep the monsters at bay
The predator has become the prey
Do you find purpose
On the way down to the bowels
Of hell?
If we all must die
Then why can't we be kinder
To make it count
Everyone you see is going
to cease to exist.
Isn't that enough
To send out a smile
A hug
Rub of the shoulders
Something to say you get it?

To Do something to make all of
This confusion have a bit of meaning?
We are born with just enough
Intelligence to know it's not fair
But within that comes
Acceptance that everyone
Faces the same fate.
There is no escaping.
Only the realization
that all that is will cease to be
And we are only left with

THE WINDS OF TIME

The winds of time
Had scattered the youth
From his weathered face.
Then vanished without even
A quick dishonest brush
Against lips too mad
To whisper an objection
Her beauty hid dark secrets
Juxtaposed against her
tousled flaxen hair
Was an absence of light,
a tenebrosity that ensnared
Any semblance of molecules
from stars that had mistakenly
Grown too cold
rejected by the heavens
Becoming lost souls trapped
With a black hole for a heart.
Some find pity for such wretchedness
They regrettably become prey
A morsel to dine upon
A stomach to never be filled
undividable from its need to devour
anything of substance
Unable of not leaving a reminder
A residue of desolation
never to leave the doorstep
Since the emptiness is never-ending
The self-loathing ever-present
The cloak and dagger
Next to whatever door
They chose to walk through

That blighted morning.
The masks easily available
Like colored straws in a diseased drawer
Whatever bright grotesque color that's needed
To distract an unsuspecting bird
To make it colorful
To make it count
Then Catch them
in a crushing exploitation
And leave no trace of who
or what they used to be
Just a barren wasteland
Undressed of its golden fields
Warm rolling exuberant lushness
Now is quiet with stoic devastation.

AH SHE CRIES POEM

Ah she cries at night
When she thinks no one can hear
But today was too much
And her young face was bathing
In her unfair pain.
We worry about children drowning in a bathtub
We never think of them drowning
in their own suffering of another's doing
To say life isn't fair
Is to bring a yawn to bear fruit
But to become resigned to this
Is to carry around a decaying past
I want to take her pain
Add it to my own
I'm past the point where trauma
Affects me like it used to
It's like I'm watching a movie
And I can't be bothered
To pay attention to the details anymore
It's all the same
Ends the same
Not one gets out alive
And somehow it just makes it easier
Easier to deal with the tremors
My body betraying me like
Most men I have dated
Or I have them.
I'm no Angel but someone too stubborn
To give in to the easiest solution.
Even though I used to be
way more easily swayed.
How to make her life less fucked up

Is beyond my mind's capacity
But I try.
Little smiles
Ringing up credit card debt
Who's going to track down
The dead to collect that?
Just add it to my tab
Along with the medical bills
And student loans
I don't need any of it anymore
Simplicity is simply Simple
The beauty of this hellscape
I've been wandering through
The last couple of years, decades, or whatever
time that seems more and more less relevant
Especially the in-between parts of where it begins and
where it untimely ends,
Is stumbling into her
A girl who could be my daughter
If that would've been a different path
I have found instead the one I did
But I never wanted to pass my trauma on
And yet the wicked sense of it all
Is her, this girl full of trauma
Who needs someone to care
Like I needed someone to care
when I was her age
And no one did
And the wolves tore at my innocence
Like starved depraved prisoners
In a Siberian work camp
That's what my childhood
Brings to mind.
The brutality of being abandoned at two
The absurdity of a revolving cast
Of elaborate ignorant players
All broken but haphazardly glued back

Cracks glaring at a small blonde
Blue eyed child
Nothing happens to those children
Or so we are told.
I guess a lot of nothing did happen
At least the good parts
seem to have been forgotten
But can you forget something
That was never there?
Memory is such a biased trickery
The mind plays on our ego
Or maybe it's the other way around.
Only Death washes the sins away
Not water not grace
Why do we make people
into who they are not?
When I die say I did one good thing
And that was to be there for her
The rest I completely spaced on
And hope there aren't too many cracks.

ESOTERIC DNA

Esoteric DNA embedded in my
phantom reality
does it all look the same?
On a cellular level
is that where my soul resides?
Am I here b/c of my past
to correct what needed
to set right and learn
what was forgotten?
My eyes tried to blind themselves but even in the
darkness everything was sharp and clear as a razor
slicing through a glacial waterfall.
Is this the beauty of an intricate simulation?
Dried depths of my being
Too high to fall and rise again
Can't make a mistake
for if I do then I don't exist for a very long time.
I want to go "too early"
To a place where there is no "too late"
I want to dissolve in the outskirts of the world.
To be lost in the depths of the terrible, terrible forest.
To swallow so much silence that there would be no
words.
Poetry only, silently rocking the world, into a gentle
permeated slumber
I befriended the eagle so that it's not too horrifying if I
suddenly find myself again in his beak.
And his best is this world, the abode of mad men…

MILES TO GO

Miles to go before I sleep
…endless fall
downwards
no sound
no rush
brain chills
 here
then not
fear a foe
survive winter
 head first
 icy water
 confusion
emptiness
fullness
weighing a cause
 a knee bending.
Around symbolism
 runs meaning
a Spinozism of circles
spinning ideas.
the spinsterhood
weaving another burden
on a back-breaking
 is the absolute in
not the reality out?

MAGIC HAPPENS

Magic happens in your eyes
A home that used to be my own
Is now trespassing should I visit
Violence once introduced
Is never in your past
But with your every step.
Hesitation, the frost heaving should
everything crumble underneath.
In the movies
Tv shows
The father is always remorseful
Asking for forgiveness
Telling his daughter how
Things were harder without her.
How he's so happy she's there now.
Would've it been so hard
to say those words?
Would've it been the worst thing?
Instead of drawing our rusty swords
To battle on the silent battlefield
Upon fallen memories of what had been.
Scattered tattered layers is the reality
Imprisoned to life's chameleonic variables.

A POEM AT 2 AM IN A BAR IN FAIRBANKS ON A DARE-AN IVORY& RAVEN LOVE AFFAIR

For what it was worth
her skin Ivory-snow white
hair like a forgotten sunset
and there was the darkness,
Raven and screeching like a northern wind
reminding all that winter is calling
and will not stop swirling,
singing the notes of whiteness.
Hey, kiss me once again, love?
I'll be your tormented bi-polar angel
screaming into self-denial.
I'll lick your feathers thoroughly
and spread them like a dessert
upon a mind impeded with desire.
That only see what is never immaculate and forever
then untouched.
As long as the brain is deterred we can prance like mad
devils
beneath an unwise moon and forget that tomorrow
actually meant that much and never came to pass.
But kiss me in the morning
lick the honeydew from my frozen fingertips.
I will bring you down...down into a return that has no
beginning just...
an endless end.

Tossing...falling...deep into her arms
there could be salvation
if only her disturbed angles were not eating the flesh
from her now motionless devils.

83

YOU LEFT ME

You left me in fear
In the sand club
Memories like fine particles
Scrapping too gently
through your calloused fingers
Thicken layers of skin
Kept your heart hidden
You claim it was enough
But what lied underneath your feet
Meant more to me than
That sky above your unbending head
Nothing could break you
Even the bruises on my skin
Burning mementos
The smoke follows me
Into my dreams
My nostrils filled
With burning ashes
Of who I once was
And still, you never looked down
As I choked on your
Uncorrected mistakes
That punished innocence
Nor did you ever completely
 close your stained fist
To stem what was left
Of broken simplicity
How to be a child again
When all was taken
Before awareness
Even began whispering
In the back hidden corners of

A naive mind
Still wandering the endless dark halls
Trying to find unlocked doors
That haven't been bolted
from within.
Dream sometimes comes
with his master key
But only for a tease
Before daytime monsters
Steal back their claim.

THE CLOUDS ARE COMING MAMA

The clouds are coming
For me mama
Trying to dance them away
But the purple-greyness of being
Is swinging my way
I see the blue
Not of my soul
But of the sky
Trying to peek through
To remind me
Nothing stays the same
But this heaviness
Won't let me breathe
Won't let me be
Enchanted by my presence
I'm the Queen & King of the Ball
Swaying hips
Wine soaked lips
Trying to make it
Just one more fucking day
One more last hooray
 let's make it count
Before the sheets are stripped bare
And there's no one left to care

THE DEATH OF A STRIPPER

"PRNSIS" BAYINNA BALLARD

ABOUT THE POET: "PRNSIS" BAYINNA BALLARD

"PRNSIS" Bayinna Ballard is the daughter of Gail and Earnest Ballard. After nearly 8 years of marriage, they split up and went their separate ways. While in elementary school, Bayinna thought writing was the best way to express herself, as she did not see it as a possible means of expression. Entertainment, while it was a huge part of who she was for many years, was neither often positively reinforced nor looked down on. The cultivation of her artistic side, combined with academia, was neither often positively reinforced nor looked down on. Both parents are now together in heaven, PRNsis never forgot the last words of encouragement given to her by both of them: "write a book" and "I should have encouraged you more in your gifts."

When Gail and Earnest separated, PRNsis found herself at Fulton Elementary School on Skyline Drive in southeast San Diego. In an upper-middle-class Black neighborhood, the neighbors were nothing like the military-housing neighbors she was used to—multicultural, accepting, and kind to the newbies. This school was a magnet school, and the teachers encouraged students to explore writing, gymnastics, or technical outlets to help them blossom and discover their talents. One day, she was in class, and for some reason, she decided to write a poem. It was a sexually charged poem that had references to fireworks and a boy and a girl kissing. To gain some popularity in class, the poem was passed around, but when the teacher got hold of it, it was like the fireworks were defective. Gail was embarrassed, Earnest was not happy, and PRNsis was put on punishment.

The writing bug never left—it became a private way to talk to God and vent emotions. While PRNsis's exact style remains undefined, inner renewal has brought fresh energy to her writing. Her parents' last words—full of encouragement, apologies, and loving reminders that she can achieve anything—mark a pivotal moment: she now writes openly, freed from fear, and shares new joy with her husband, Jesse Bannon.

PRNsis's entertainment resume is extensive, though less so in writing. She is an on-camera TV host, executive producer, and red-carpet host. She prides herself on ad-lib questions, spontaneous conversations, and occasional freestyle rap—for fun, not for sure, as she says. It's her hope to write a memoir and children's books, which she and a close friend created several years ago—stories about triumph, awkward friendships, and the special love of a parent.

Something PRNsis loves to remember when writing is that God is everywhere. God loves to see the passion and the courage to be on the front lines with the gifts given. The best time to write is when you do it.

SYNOPSIS

THE DEATH OF A STRIPPER: CONSTANTLY REBRANDING, TRASH TALKIN AND FINALLY LETTING GO

I'm not always and have never been positively sure about the path I am on. I know I'm not alone, and I'm sure that I never was, except that time when I literally went to jail. Nobody ever said it was easy to walk away from a career that afforded me opportunities and the luxuries of travel, and that paid all my bills on time. I always thought the choices I made were the right ones. But now it seems like all I did was take everything I knew and just quit. I mean, I just gave it all up, and while I stayed where I was, I also moved, and I grew as a person, as a wife, and as a child of God. Have you ever thought you were who you wanted to be, only to realize you're not anywhere close to that person?

I have not always taken the steps to finish the things I started, but the one thing I started and never stopped is being sober, and dreaming, trying new jobs, and other things, like this. I've been hoping too, and I've been chasing after the one thing that gives me, at least in my mind and heart, purpose. I have realized that I am a team player and a leader with great ideas. I am creative and have a beautiful, creative mind. I also have a vast network of people whom I consider friends, but they are really acquaintances. Despite these strengths, I lack self-esteem and get caught up in my insecurities. I thought I had people to support me and walk alongside me, but I came to see that it was a figment of my imagination. These writings are my expression of self-care, self-love, and self-worth, and they stand as a testimony of my acceptance of my own reality.

These writings are the most authentic and truthful thoughts I have, maybe not daily- but often. They are about what's going on in my head; they are my conclusions, based on the actions of others and how

I see myself in my community. There are a lot of people who know me, but I wonder if they see that I have trauma and hurt. These writings are my understanding of what people really think of me, based on the conversations and interactions I have had. These writings give a little access and understanding into my mind for those who care, or not, for those who know me, and also know that I know my purpose. Like most humans, I have lost sight of it at times. I gave in to the games and the mindful tricks of others' opinions, and I also gave in to defeat. I gave in to my own fear, my own procrastination, and my belief that nobody would want to work with me. I am not a high-maintenance person, but they can't see how hurtful it is to be mocked or talked about. Yes, I have a high level of sensitivity. Of course, it's only one side of the story, and I know that. But these writings allow me to share my pain, get it off my chest, and use my words on paper instead of a public clapback. I'm grateful for the opportunity because my Mom told me to do it a week before she passed. This is me getting my toe wet, but it's for her and for my Dad.

THEY DONE #SOULDOUTTOSOCIALS

Everybody gets a like, heart, or comment
Unless you don't get a like, heart, or comment

I keep telling myself social media is not real
but why do I keep seeing shit that is pretty clear
And it's not me tellin' a lie
some actions of my closest friends be keeping me inside
My head
My heart

What's going is real and what my eyes read and see
You can't tell me some BS like I took it too personally
Get over it
Forealz tho

Y'all wanna act like sensitivity is a mutha fuckin' plague
like it's too contagious to be around me or even
like, comment, and leave a heart
by whatever I post and the comments I make.

This is some bullshit
every 6 months I shut it down because when I be myself
don't nobody really like me…

One nigga even told me once to my face
"We can't use yo service because it's not good enough to
be in our space," That same dude showed up to events
dropping my name, no invite, no hesitation, and hearts
and comments on all his thangs

Another nigga told me straight up I care too much,
and I want to be everybody's friend.
It's a waste of time, and I be trippin'

This shit really happened and some other stuff I need
not say but maybe everybody doesn't deserve a heart,
like, or comment
But I am somebody
If you're my friend and I say something
don't be blatantly ignoring me
that shit make you a fake
Even if you only say it with an emoji
it's better than being the only comment left out like I'm
so funky

You know what?
Twist that.
I am the shit.
Ahead of my time
And I know
I be makin' waves
I been a trendsetter since 12th grade.

TALKING MYSELF OFF THE LEDGE

Too often
I be in my head and the thoughts and questions I have
I found myself
Questioning who I am
Asking for forgiveness
Not being heard
Misunderstood
Emotional
This has been a problem for me for a long time

In elementary school
the black girls always jumped me
In high school
I was not popular and the black girls always talked
trash about how I dressed

Not to sound like an angry black woman,
But damn, why am I constantly being ignored
I thought that sisters and brothers in the black
community
Are committed to lifting up
Are supposed to walk alongside
Are supposed to bring value
and help put ideas into action
Then again, I may be confused in my thinking
All black people are supposed to do is be who they are

Truthfully,
I am trying to use discernment
in what they do and say to me

Is it beneficial or is it not
The question is also a symbol of my commitment to
being the best I can
To also stay in my lane and grow into the PRNsis I am
called to be
Because no matter what they do or say to me, imma
black girl too

Get yo ass off yo high horse
Use discretion and not force
When you realize that you failed
You kept me at your side
I had a role and a position
With a title and authority
You think you're so smart
You can't even see the mistakes you make
And everybody sees
You keep trying but it's me who makes the waves

Sit yo ass down and stop scrolling
That shit ain't real and has nothing to do with you
You always act like you supposed to be
everywhere and do everything
Chick, you got it all messed up
everybody sees you
Playing that Jesus music
in situations they think it don't match.
Continue producing events that are non-secular
The reality is you ain't no regular-degular
Set apart is what you are,
And you have no reason thinking
You're not a super-duper shining star

SPICY BLUEBERRY JAM AND PEANUTBUTTA

I loved me
I was so happy to be me
When I was doing me,
there wasn't nothin' anybody could tell me
I was hot like a jalapeño
And more like jelly than jam
Because my booty shook
And then I met a man
Many there were when I met him,
and along the way something in me had changed
I stood by the sliding door and heard a voice say to me,
"This is the man I want to stay."
Nine years later, he still adores me
Since I heard that voice, the shakin' stopped
And got thicker than a jar of peanutbutta
And that man is my jam
With God as our rock
This is why we hot
Spicy blueberry
And peanutbutta,
Together we each otha's jam.

ON THE SIDE OF THE MOUNTAIN

There's always a great way
Always a better way
But the best way will never be easy
Like climbing the side of a mountain
Once you reach the summit
There's always a beautiful view
Once you get there you remember how you slipped
How the struggle of breathing was an affliction
How you found the perfect walking stick, but it broke
You were on the trail with others
But now you're all alone
And when you finally reach the summit
You realize the mistake of forgetting your phone
Only you can see the view
You cannot share the experience
Now each breath is joy; still you're breathing
Assistance is necessary but it also can fail
The journey on the side of the mountain
Can be lonely but if you keep going
There is still a happy ending
Moral and truth is,
Resilience never fails

MY MEDIOCRE CHOKER

There was a time when I was traveling all over the place
Living intercontinentally, that was the life.

But I never really had the assurance's that truly mattered
And that's an internal strife.

financially I balled out-
on a budget
Internally I was crying out and dying to fit in
Not sure why people think I'm mediocre.

I never wanted to be somethin' that I was not
and for this reason
Finally, I see
By following the narrow road got me farther than
The likes
The numbers
and the followers indeed.

Today I admit
that is never what I truly thought

I'm more of the woman I used to be
less of the friend I was
Yearning for acceptance to be included
wondering why they don't pick me for that spot

Let me say to those who looked and said so foolishly:
Mediocre that's all she be doing.

I trust in God
I believe in His plans for me
Because my dreams
My passion, my purpose
It's for His glory.
He is the reason why
I do what I do

I'MRUBBAYOUISGLUE

I tried to and I told 'em
about how I was lost
there wasn't anybody to help me
I was bold and said things
That were probably true

You know that shit be scary

I tried to let 'em know that the way they be messing
around with the spirits and the principalities
They better stop because it's not the way to be
But they don't care
What God
say these days
that has no relevance
they done tried to and told me this several times too
but idgaf because
I am like rubber and they like glue
no more sniffing, drinkin', and smokin' for me
Now all the drama
bounces off me and stick to you boo hoo hoo

I'M NOT GONNA...

I'm not gonna be
What you think I am.
I'm only doing what I can
I don't understand why there's
Resistance and shade

You smile and support until
My ideas are good and change
I'm not over here trying to bitch and moan
It's the accepting part
That I should be focusing on

I'm not gonna be mad because
I must have done something good
I feel blocked and totally misunderstood.
It may sound like I am salty
I won't disagree but that doesn't mean
I'm alone in my faulting
In preparation for what is to come
And let His will be done

BACKSLIDE

When I was dancin'
In the prime of my life
I went to jail
I got saved
I think about that period of my life
I wonder where I would be now if
I didn't backslide

If I didn't feed my flesh
trusting in a man
to make it easy
to pass the time
someone to blame for the night I choose to backslide

I think about all the miracles God used me for
what if I could have kept those gifts
let God continue to open doors
Where would I be right now
I wonder and often I get mad
where are my miracles now that I changed God
Or do I only get one chance
was I special only when I got busted
I'm not now that I have learned
at a point in my life, I could hear you speak to me
And today my connection to you is a bit blurred
Everybody knew you were in the strip club with me
you did the most and
I stopped eating the word and
I lost the closeness of the Holy Ghost
I admit it was
My absurd actions
The enemy is still trying me

You know my thoughts and heart
Lead me, guide me
I recommit to You
Your will, your way
Will you ever trust me
Enough to bring back that Holy Ghost fire
I promise I won't
ever
again
backslide

THE DEATH OF BAINA KANDI

I killed Baina Kandi when it was time
They broke her and bruised her
she stayed alive
Baina Kandi never thought she would die
Before that, she was Elexis
Trouble came, and she cried out for something fresh

Baina Kandi touched so many people's lives.
Those were special days and even more special nights
Then they came again and this time made her cry
They dragged her name and stole her things,
And Baina Kandi liked so many of them
And it was this time she realized

For a fresh and new rebirth,
Baina Kandi had to die.
So with the help of Heavenly Father,
Just to keep the good parts of her alive,
She cried out, "If I am yours, change my name! I
recommit my life!"

It took some time, but today, people call her PRNsis Bay
It's a calling, for I am chosen to Pray Right Now sis.
Thanks be to God
That is the name He gave,
and of which I will forever be defined.

REAL DREAMS

May blooms are visions
Petals come down later
Found out truth and fled

RECLAIMING MY WOMANHOOD

JULIE WHATMOUGH

ABOUT THE POET: JULIE WHATMOUGH

JULIE WHATMOUGH IS A NATURE LOVER, Army veteran, and peace advocate. As a Moon Circle facilitator, she encourages women to take care of their mental, physical, and spiritual well-being. Julie is a member of the Foundlynx Writing Group, where she has been creating *Rising in The Darkness*, a collection of poems about healing and loving with PTSD, and exploring her memoir *Unspoken Shrapnel*, a field guide of shame, secrecy, and trauma in the military.

Her poem *I Am an Acorn* was published in the Anchorage Daily News.

SYNOPSIS: RECLAIMING MY WOMANHOOD

Reclaiming My Womanhood shares the process of transmuting pain into empowerment by taking ownership of my mind and body and rewriting my story. These poems reflect my experience of sexual trauma from assault and, to some extent, cultural indoctrination. I offer the raw emotions that came with facing my demons and speaking my truth. To me, this collection explores shared stories, limiting beliefs, and the battles women face around the world. In the wake of pressures to conform, to be silent, to forgive and forget without accountability or justice, to move on for the sake of superficial harmony, we come face to face with ourselves and a choice. A choice to allow ourselves to heal, to change our lives, and connect with others by feeling deeply and letting ourselves be seen and held. *Reclaiming My Womanhood* is a story of self-love.

WOMAN'S BODY

Soft touch
strong
curvaceous
a rebellion to
society; to bathe
in pleasure

Who permits deep
joy, or
pleasure?

Desecrated, the collective
pain body feeds on
struggle.

Break free!

Be free!

Touch yourself and
break your heart open,
feel the essence
of your soul.

Embody your Self.
Leave nothing behind.

INHERENTLY

I AM
lovable,
worthy of respect

And trapped in this cage.

Mind closing down,
going black,
is there…
a witness?

Alone, I'm alone,
with a surrounding presence
and can I quite
escape?

Tears in my eyes.
Silent like a doe in the dark.

I should only have to say NO — once.

CRYPTIC

I open myself to share

But only riddles fall out of me.

Broken boundaries made me a spy
Dressed in passwords and in hiding,

Secrecy was my middle name.
"You won't find me now!" I claimed
Behind my walls and gates.
Drawbridge, secret tunnel.
Dead ends, and mysteries.

"How do I get out?" I cry.
But no one hears my plea.

SCREAM

I hate him.

And if I was to define,
it would be too many

And the time too often.

And once is already
more than too often

But still.
The rage builds
and it deepens with
the familiarity of the story.

One that is not just mine, but shared.

One that does not
have to be told
because it is known

by the thousands,
the millions of women,
and men

who were robbed
and given no way to proceed.

With no voice to tell their story the pain grows.
A burn and aching inside.
No choice but to scream.

THE EARTH
CAN HOLD YOU

Bring your anger.

Feel the heat inside rising,
red filling your body, up to your eyes
past the top of your head. Rage.

Followed by stopping.
Feel the Earth, cool beneath you.
Containing vast bodies of water.
Soothing, energy rising up through your body.
Can you allow an exchange?
Can you let the anger drain down to the ground,
into the dirt, and let the earth
hold your frustration, disappointment, heartbreak.

Breathe in, and out.
Transmutation is possible.

Can you let yourself be held?

GRIEF CIRCLE

I sit cross-legged
palms pressed into the Earth
connecting my breath
to great mother.

Asking her to take my sorrow,
to receive my grief.

I release from my hands
all the holding on.
My weight sinks into my fingertips,
my wrists, my arms
feeling the steady embrace of her love.

The never-ending support and stability of a mother's
consistent presence.

Her response, a gentle reminder.

I am strong enough to stand,
and brave enough to lean on this
circle of women.

To cry and be held, and to hold.

To remain awake
with the awareness of compassion.

We connect to feel hope.
And remember we are all children of Mother Earth.

TO MY MOTHER

I love you.
And I know
you didn't mean to
shame my body.
Telling me to cover
my skin was
an act of protection.
An ask of concern,
and fear
of the world 'out there.'
Of people who
wish to harm
or degrade.

Though it is not possible to
degrade one who is inherently invaluable.

I recognize your wish,
that your love could
be a cloak of safety,
and I,
never hurt.

But fabric doesn't stop those
who want to cause pain.
It does not stop those
who believe a relationship
means ownership.

But the idea
I should hide myself,
did stop me

from believing in my power.

It did raise questions
of my value and how it
could change.

It did separate me
from the ownership and autonomy of
my body.

My body.
And I love you all the more for your heart
and desire to keep me safe.

And thank you for your trust as I step
into my essence and
choose what I reveal.

EVERYTHING HAS ITS OWN TIME

I am my own night and day.
I am the riverbanks and the storm that overflows them.
I am the shadow in the forest.
I am the mountain in the sky blanketed in crystal white.

I am Persephone the child
and the Royalty of the Underworld.
I am Athena poised and ready.
I am Kali giving birth in the wake of my destruction.
I am the foundation and the house.

Stop. Breathe. Release.
Everything takes its own time.
I am the magick and the divine.

WHEN I AM READY

When I am ready I will stretch my eyes
my hands will reach out
And my heart will receive.

When I am ready I will move my body
I will undulate like the seas
Full body motion, I move as I please.

I am an ocean of unexplored depths
When I am ready I will do as I please.

UNLEASHED

I have begun to unleash myself fully
To release myself with abandon.
To completely let go and run into my truth.
Full flower essence kissed by the dew of the Star.
Sun in my hair and dancing with the rain.
Laughter through tears and smiling till it hurts.

Not overwhelmed by the power in me, but in deep
embodiment, harnessing my energy.
Not a boat in the storm but the storm itself.
Raw, untamed, ruthlessly making way,
creating the path with intention,
removing all the ill-fitting parts.
A green pasture growing in full bloom
No such thing as weeds and no weed-whacking

A tenderness of gentle hands, planting down, and a
whisper of love, silky sweet as it slides into my ears,
swirls around my head, and slips i
nto my heart.

The center of all creation.
Devotion. Peace. Truth. Harmony.

Love - beyond the niceties and dream promises.
A sense of belonging.
A sense of place.
Of acceptance.
Of yes!

Yes!!

I open my heart, my mouth moves and I moan;
full body ground as I extend beyond myself.
Ahhh. Deep sigh. Contentment.
I am all that I am.
I cannot be contained.

MEASURES OF MORTALITY

ERIC GORDON JOHNSON

ABOUT THE POET: ERIC GORDON JOHNSON

ERIC GORDON JOHNSON was born in Fairbanks in 1948 and raised in Anchorage, Alaska. He earned an MFA in Creating Writing in poetry at the University of Alaska, Anchorage in December 2020. He won an honorable mention for a short story in the University of Alaska, Anchorage and Anchorage Daily News writing contest. He has published poems and a short story in Cirque Literary Journal. He published a memoir in Anchorage Remembers published by 49Writers. He also has several broadsides published by 49Writers. He has published poetry in the Alaska Humanities Forum. He is a member of Drumlin Poets, Poetry Parley and 49Writers. He has taught poetry classes for Opportunities for Lifelong Education.

SYNOPSIS

MEASURES OF MORTALITY

Ten poems related to death and the relationship to animals.

GOD OF ANTS

Back when I was just a little boy
I'd search the woods with my dog
to find bugs and other living toys.
I'd bust up some old and rotten log,

then take a stick to make the crazed ants run
this way and that and all around
to move their eggs to another dead stump
crawling through cranberry bushes on the ground.

One day I decided to stage a tragic act.
Taking an old and rusted tin can, I chose
for actors one red ant and another black
and tried to make them fight in close.

I thought to play god from above,
but the ants just ignored my love.

WHAT HAD I DONE?

Wanting the forbidden
I whacked the flying dragonfly
with a baseball bat.
Silence lay like a mausoleum
in bright sunlight.
I held the dead bug
and stared at what I had done.
Perfectly preserved
the hooked tail
the translucent gasoline tinted wings
that no more would fly.
And losing my childhood fascination
I pitched it in the bushes.
Misplacing my essence
I had slain this little messenger.

MAN BEAR

we gorged on watermelon that night
the red juice running down our cheeks
tossing the rinds in the latrine
later we were wakened by our elders
and told to stay in our tents
so as not to see
what was being done
and of course we peeked
through the boreal summer's midnight twilight
to see the terrified animal
surrounded by our men betters
standing on its hind legs
as the shot pierced its bared chest
and it screamed like a man

BLACK BEAR SOW

She presented herself
with cubs through
spruce and birch,
choosing not to bolt
like other bears
that spotted me.
Instead, she seemed content
to let me stand
watering my morning lawn
as she towed the two
toward me.
She brought them
over the hose
between my spraying
and the blaring pump
down by the pond.
She shooed her brood
up a cottonwood.
They scrambled branchless, up
the rough bark until after
resting on the first thick branch,
they climbed to the top
swaying in the thin breeze
before sliding down the trunk
then climbing in the air again and again.
When I went in,
she brought them down
and took them up the mountain.

The hiker told the reporter later
she had charged him
and he had to shoot her.

HUMAN PURPOSES

In stark winter
wolves bring down
an injured cow moose.
Blood spatters on snow.

In summer thick smoke
from a forest fire
caused by likely lightning,
drives hares and a bull moose before it.

These contain no catastrophe.

Only the human animal
undertakes to exploit nature,
subduing it for his own purposes,
slaughtering hundreds of bears
in the hope of gorging on moose
creating the tragedy
of a barren land.

NATURE'S WAYS

Bit tulips lie clipped,
fresh dead, no decay,
a hare had bit,
before humans could pick.
But up the mountainside,

no moose, no hare,
disturbs alpen blooms:
elfin shooting star,
ruminating monkshood,

squat dwarf violet,
and placid glacial avens,
on high-clouded peak
that stands in its own presence.

HALFWAY ROUND TWO-DAY TRAIL

through the back-country of Crow Pass
past Raven Glacier
across the boulder piles
and over gorge's bridge
nothing human for miles and miles
plunging through waist-high grass that
hid my tripping feet.
An electric pain stings
from bees between sweaty thighs.

And I see a grizzly lumber
onto the trail fifty yards ahead.

Don't run. Don't
run. The bear would chase.
Fight or play dead?

Backing down the trail
and stepping behind
a short scrawny spruce--
if he wants me, this tree provides
no protection.

Dropping my pack from my back,
fishing for pepper spray, I fumble,
knocking the cannister out
onto the trail on a miss-grab--
too close, no time
to retrieve, my
only defense

gone.

Muscles ripple under
tawny fur. Long sharp
claws ripping my
imagined face. I smell
the stench
of his breath.

Then the wet black bulging nose passes.
ignoring my presence, wanting only
the right-of-way,
taking it on down the trail.

And as he leaves my sight,
I feel again my inner thigh
with its prayerful pain.

SCOTT'S POND

We watched a bull moose
on our lawn for two weeks
barely changing position
as it stood lifting one front leg
and then the other
when not lying down
sleeping, its head propped on
one antler, floating above the frost
frozen grass.

A cow moose and later another
bull entered the lawn's sphere
but our moose would not entertain
any notion of recognition.

The third week, it slowly moseyed
down to the pond,
named for a dead boy,
broke ice with its hoof
and drank water.

Two more weeks passed
of wandering around our house
when it withdrew behind
a stand of trees by the pond
and died as skaters skated around
its frozen faintly reeking carcass
as wind waved through the alders
chiming the ice rimed branches.

Ravens and magpies pecked out its eyes

and chased a coyote back across the pond
and hassled a young bald eagle,
but did not deter bears
we could not see behind trees
as they snuck through the woods
on a well pawed trail in the snow
and tore the bones apart
and hauled them away.

Now nothing is left except
two ribs and some fur.

DESCENDING NEAR PEAK'S SOUTHERN SLOPE

After hiking the afternoon
two ravens circle above me.
They are met by many more
until nearly fifty, gamboling,
gyring ever higher,
dipping, falling back towards earth
calling to each other
with glugging clucking water music.

At first I think it's me
they choose to play above,
and move me with their motion,
but no: only the rising
thermals of the sun lift them up.
And when they tire of their play
They continue home beyond the peak
and I on down the mountainside.

MIDDLE FORK

I stand above misted trees that cling
to cliffs that shine from the gorge
with a powerful peace. A muffled rumble
calls from the unseen stream, spirit of
an unsunned shadow under leaves. Earth's stony
gash below my feet, an oracle,
nothing to mankind. It is earth's breath,
today ignored. Yet its jealous
grasping tears at the heart
amid blood-red salmon berries.
The silent swoop of a great horned owl
floats over the chasm,
a quiet ghost with extended
claws, gray feathers aflutter in its
wind. Flight mastered
without demand but to the depths below
where waits the unsuspecting hare.
There will come a time when
I step down and count myself
a part of this and join
the god talk of the gorge.

FINDING YOUR BEARINGS

ZOE WOODS

ABOUT THE POET: ZOE WOODS

ZOE WOODS IS a white queer poet, naturalist, and outdoor educator. Her work explores our relationship with nature through the lens of wilderness, wildness, and humanness. She has work that will be published by Beyond Words Magazine and Beyond Queer Words in 2025. Originally from Colorado, she is now based in Alaska.

SYNOPSIS
FINDING YOUR BEARINGS

Like so many before me, I came to Alaska searching for something or, just as likely, running from something. I left the Lower 48 like a thief in the night, abandoning my home, a relationship, and everyone I'd ever known. This collection follows that journey to Alaska and the subsequent wonder and reckoning I experienced over the course of my first year. It traces wide-eyed naiveté that eventually gives way to a deeper appreciation of the landscape. As I try to orient myself to this place, each season yields new observations and realizations. In these incredible wild spaces, I reckon with deeper truths about myself, as well as the changing world around me. From the Chugach mountains and Denali tundra to the tide pools of Homer and waves of the Prince William Sound, the natural world served as my writing desk. This collection is a love letter to the landscapes of Alaska, as well as an unfinished story. Alaska will keep evolving in a warming world, and so will I.

NORTH STAR

I was following my own north star
And I thought it was leading me to the heavens

But instead,
It led me back to earth

At the beck
And call
Of the raptors
And the rapids
Of the tides
And the tidepools
Of the wilderness
And the wilds

When your compass points true north,
All the way north,
Who are you to deny it?

CANDY SHOP

Tide pools on a rainy May morning,
I am reminded of a shop of sweet curiosities
Ribbons of pulled-taffy seaweed
Among gummy orange anemones

With childlike glee, I poke
Lime green pouches
That explode underfoot
And feel lozenge smooth mussels
Polished by the lapping of the sea

I can almost taste
Chewy strips of strawberry kelp
Sea stars bulging like ripe fruit
And rock candy urchins

With a child's eye
The earth becomes a buffet
As the original elders say
When the tide is out
The table is set

ASPIRATION

Old Faithful spurts from beneath the waves
She's slippery like a hard-boiled egg
Her saddle shimmers
A freshly washed car in the sun

We collectively gasp
As if we were preparing to dive ourselves
But we are already submerged
In awe
In wonder

We inhale sharply
Hoping she might take us down with her
Just to glimpse the other face
Of this terra infirma

TAPESTRY

On these nights with neither sun nor moon
I long to see
the weaver of the universe

Thin threads connecting the cosmos
Against a deep indigo sky

I'm reminded of those long past
Who sat under these same skies
Marveled at the intricacies of creation
Nursed by awe of infinity
Cradled in a tapestry woven from eons of light

Each shower across that universal womb
Reminding us how fleeting we are
Just bursts of light
In an infinite sky

IN THE FALL

The tundra bruises against
The thump of winter
Like a knee bumped into a table

Rich purples and reds bloom
Fading with the icy salve of a first frost
Yellowing each passing day

Fireweed snow blows away with the wind
Summer's Irish goodbye
Leaving behind only a coffee ring
Soon to be wiped clean

WHEN I LEFT YOU FOR ALASKA

You told me you hoped I'd grow roots
so deep that even the black gum trees were envious
And then you said

The Alaska state tree is the Sitka spruce
A tree which has shallow, ledge-gripping roots
Nothing more to say about these, just a fact for you.

But did you know?
That the Sitka spruce
Forgoes deep roots
For sky-grasping branches
Its needles breathe water from the air
Sipping the constant fog and rain

And maybe it was not roots I was looking for
But to be sustained by the rain
Freedom to breathe in life itself

CPR

Laying down on a bed of moss
Gazing upwards
Tree branches waltz
Their leaves fluttering with the breeze

Cedar sighs and I deeply inhale
We are locked in a sweet embrace
Green, fresh lips pressed to mine
She breathes life into me and I into her
A tender mouth to mouth remedy

The sky presses down on my sternum
The weight of hope
I am
Alive once more

AFTER SPRING BREAKUP

It was here in the Sound
I learned to love again
From the earth, sea, and sky

Her love, a gust of air
Blows off the glacier
Tenderly ruffling my hair

Her love, a sun-ripened salmonberry
All nature's sweetness bundled
And left out for me to find

Her love, constant
Like the steady drizzle of rain
Showing up no matter the weather

It was here, I learned
To notice
The waterfalls flowing
Becoming ever more shy throughout the summer
The tide rising
And the glacier's smile becoming more lopsided
The whales breaching
Just wanting a taste of the world above

And surely there is no greater act of love than noticing

When I close my eyes
I feel her notice me in return
In the lapping of the waves
The whistle of the wind
The call of the wildness

She says
You are here
You are here
You are here.

FERAL LOVE

I look out from the mountaintop cradle
where I've sat to rest
Gazing at the world unfurled beneath my feet
A mosaic of valley greens and slate stones
A tapestry of blue threads and white tassels

Adoration blooms within me
Baking soda and vinegar bubbling up with ferocity
It starts in the chasm of my stomach
Tickles my sternum
Chokes up my throat
That something like this could exist still in this world
we've made
That beauty on this scale persists

Perhaps I ran away to Alaska
To prove there was some absolution
That there were indeed wild places left
I take a breath of skim milk air
A momentary respite from the grief and fear
Of fires and heat,
Drought and extinction

But
An umbrella to weather the coming storm
Heart-pounding feral love
Relentless, untamed care
That grief and fear can feed a creek
But love can sustain a flood.

MIDNIGHT / SUN

I ran away to Alaska
For the promise of an infinite wilderness
And at the top of the world
I thought I found
What I had been looking for

On the high elevation summits
I let my ghosts run off leash
Watched them race around clouds
And chase hawks back to their nests

Under the vast sky
I could finally breathe deeply
Filling my lungs to the absolute brim and
Savoring the taste like a glass of wine

In the glacial runoff
I was baptized
In that cold fire communion
Newborn into the wild

Beneath the midnight sun
My shadows disappeared
And I could dance
Without looking over my shoulder

But the midnight sun sets
And midnight began its prowl across the sky
Everything I had been running from
Found its way back to me

In the quiet of the fresh snow

My thoughts became deafening
On the icy lakes,
My composure slipped away
In the avalanche's path,
I was buried by doubts

In the long winter night
I invited my ghosts in to warm up with a cup of tea
Together
We watched the northern lights wisp across the sky
Like a match struck and blown out
Smoke from a distant cosmic fire

I was hypnotized by

The midnight sun's promises of
Shadowless daydreaming
Sunbathed escapism

But here in the midnight
I sink into the depths of myself
Finally done chasing
Finally ready for facing
Ready to learn
What lessons midnight might teach me

ONE FOOT IN THE WILDERNESS

VIVIAN FAITH PRESCOTT

CHAPTER 1
ABOUT THE POET: VIVIAN FAITH PRESCOTT

VIVIAN FAITH PRESCOTT (SHE/HER) is a bi writer, born and raised on a small island, Wrangell, Kaachxana.áak'w, in Southeast Alaska. She lives and writes at her family's fishcamp on the land of the Shtax'heen Kwáan. She's a member of the Pacific Sámi Searvi (Indigenous Sámi diaspora) and a founding member of the first LGBTQIA group on the island. She's the author of poetry, fiction and non-fiction. She's also a co-founder and co-facilitator of two Alaskan writers' groups: Blue Canoe Writers and the Drumlin Poets.

SYNOPSIS

ONE FOOT IN THE WILDERNESS

These poems depict the inner workings of anxiety and its comorbidities and their effects on the narrator's life. In poetry we should always assume the "I" is not the poet themselves. In this case, it is me, but the poet's voice is also a persona, i.e. the facetious me. Publishing these poems is a brave act for me and for the narrator too. The poems are in a relationship with the humanity of having anxiety while being a part of the natural world, specifically Alaska. Anxiety is described as a toad, a wolf, a bear, winter, dust, eyes, hair, petroglyphs, a wavelet, and a coffeeshop. My hope is that these poems will open a dialogue about anxiety and take away some of the shame that sufferer's experience.

ANXIETY IS A TOAD

I have one foot in the wilderness,
in the shallow water,
peering at a chain of bead-like eggs
as if they're floating beneath glass.

Yes, I'm forever sensing the presence
of dragon fly wings, and listening for the cry-alarm
of the yellowlegs, and the otter

slinging its body across a slick rock.
I'm in a perpetual wave-state of metamorphosing
and it's moss-soaked and muddied

as always beneath my rough skin.
But you would never know it. I am used to this life
though—
I don't remember ever not loving

a small pond or a patch of tall lake grass,
or that I would much rather
be a girl with bangs dripping
in raindrops. I should be hallowed

in the museum of Ranids. I can stand here
all day between the marsh violets and the spike-rush
and answer your question—Why?

THE DIRE

The wolf in me gnaws at everything—
like it's conversing with cackling ravens

and day-long fears as often as the alders'
pollen puffs burst across the bay in spring.

All my life, this intense state has been
an unsayable thing. Yes, I'll name it now—

anxiety. I've never been unable to reveal
my tender underside, to hand someone

my thorn-wounded paw. I'm so used to
the wide space between human and creatures

that shame recoils me into the back far corner
of my den. My instinct is to be toasty warm.

Safe. And have nothing around me with
the ability to branch-snap a startle,

or stare-eye jab itself into my spine. Sometimes,
I must convince myself the moon's albedo,

that animal staring back at me might really
be watching over me. It's how I'm supposed

to exist—casting shadows and baring my teeth.

CHECKLIST OF MISUNDERSTANDING COMORBIDITIES

☑ Comorbidities sound like I ate a whole salmon by myself & choked on salmon bones while eating the side of rice.

☑ Seems like it means I decline all the invites to everywhere— It's safer here at the edge of the sea.

☑ Seems like I don't like to fly but it's not that—there's an airport

☑ & taxi cabs, & gates, & people & people

& decisions & what if something/anything happens

& I don't know what I don't know....

☑ Seems like I've been called bitch or aloof or a troublemaker, even.

☑ Seems like I don't speak up.

☑ Seems like I speak up too much.

☑ Seems like there's always an excuse for I can't do whatever that sounds more like *the tide is going out and there's a tide pool with spiny green sea urchins I've been meaning to look at.*

☑ Try being a comorbid soul looking after two other comorbid souls— We're shared causes & walking/talking risk factors. We are distinct.

☑ One condition causes the other & sometimes I don't know which one is in the lead. So instead, I keep wandering on the beach in a spiral motion until I etch out a universal vortex pattern in big rock & become a petroglyph.

In the future, people will wonder who made the glyph.

ANXIETY INTERLUDE

The day pulses with lingering hours
as we near the solstice. I meander
in the forest around the lettuce lichen

and the gray cabbage lungwort.
I can't yet tell the difference between
these lichens because my body

is out of focus most times. Sometimes,
for me, there is no difference between
outer threats and the inner threats

—the bear floating on the periphery
through the bushes of my dreams
has been a stress warning my entire life.

But in the forest, my worries flush out,
soothing the crinkles beneath my skin,
and taming the electricity hovering

like an aural blanket, where normally
even a simple mistake can climb
with sharp-nailed cleats up my spine.

But not here—I have become dependent
on this forest, this island, for my existence.
Like the lichen, I am well adapted

to this life now. I've learned not to buckle
under, to not let these feelings intrude
and trounce the forest path.

Here, down in this valley, beneath
the ancient esker, my brand of survival
in this caper we call life is to sit

on my knees, not to summon a silent
unseen god, but to reach out—
a being to another being—join the family

of the flying squirrel, and the deer—
an invocation that considers an old
tree stump covered in fairy barf.

ANXIETY METAPHORS GOING NOWHERE

My day follows a sense that everything is rusting,
everything is a windswept drowning,
is a wild running
back to something I cannot name
except to call it fucking hell.

I love to watch British murder shows
with the CC turned on where they
swear our American words
like they're simply breathing in-and-out.
No one notices.

My anxiety is drowned in afternoon tea
just like that. There are words and studies
for this sensation moving across me
like clouds billowing over the island.

I feel like I might need closed captions
on my life to describe myself clearly to others.

            (anxiety) could be in parentheses

because this weight is unspoken, un-muddied
by spring's reach. Goddamn, I hate the sentiment—
It is what it is—because mine is a perpetual wavelet
pushing and pushing against the seawall.

WHAT TO KNOW BEFORE STOPPING MEDICATIONS

The swans, geese, gulls and ravens
entertain us, flocking to our beach

as if we were a sanctuary—
the two poet / three dog unit

spinning dizzy in our own sphere of hope,
just trying to survive the gloom

of impending winter. But what is hope
but an anxious smudged position on a nautical chart,

we've market lightly as if it's somewhere
over there, beyond a stack of rocks,

in the bend of cove, a place we've yet to arrive.
We don't seem to have hope yet,

because doom still reeks. Our hands and feet
now feel the nip of winter like little bites

trying to kill us in increments.
I have formally withdrawn my hope for hope.

My cries of despair are now chimes clinking
in the wind, heard over rough waves.

Maybe, though, your cries and our cries

can mingle together like notes rising
in a whale song above the sea.

HAIRWORK

Rapunzel, Rapunzel pull out your hair—
One strand for mourning, one for a keepsake,
one for the family tree.

Rapunzel Rapunzel, was a little girl once,
a five-year-old me, not yet locked in a tower,
but witch-shut inside a family fable

and told how I was a child who rocked
in the corner—rock-rock-pull, rock-rock-pull.
Around the world, there is hairwork, strands

weighted with wire, woven into braids,
designs tying knots, bowing a heart,
shaping leaves and lyres, even wrapping wrists.

But the little child me, a sad girlwork for sure,
snuggled with her baby doll and tore out its hair.
I pilled fuzz in my pockets, rolled fur in my fingers

for magic making, for instead-of-a-hug,
for wishing for my momma, who had poofed
herself away out of town one day, and left

little Rapunzel me, playing with a bald doll,
inside a storybook with the pages yanked out
and slapped back by a new stepmother.

I'd like to end the fable here with a prince
or princess climbing up a long braid
when the girl grows up, but it ends with a chant

I've been charming to myself every day
and for years—Rapunzel, Rapunzel,
cut your damn hair, scissor a skippy pixie cut,

shear above the ears. Shock it short-short,
lop the locks, so, when life thrills you to reach up
toward your head, you can trill out to yourself—

Don't go there. Don't go there. Girl, the tower's
toppled and the grim's gone, and you've lived
your defiance by a hairsbreadth,

unbroken as an earthen ringfort, charmed as a verse—
Girl, you've outlasted the spell—when everyone
in the realm thought you wouldn't, you survived.

MIGHT AS WELL
BE A COFFEE SHOP
ON THE MOON

No coffee for the fretful—
latte, cappuccino, frappuccino, frappe, venti, grande
no clue
one shot or two
coffee is a stimulant
not small comforts

    just don't ask me questions
    I'll freeze—

because I'm lost in the jargon—
macchiato, cold brew
steamed milk, milk foam

    people know things I don't know

the coffee shop is an atmosphere I can't breathe in
& it's like I'm walking in there with my astronaut helmet on
& my mike is muted
but they say coffee shops are designed to be comforting
& relaxed with background music
a sea of tranquility

    except for those of us
    who avoid coffee shops

don't try to convince me there's glee in social interactions
designed to boost your mood & how the act of ordering

& interacting with the barista makes a connection
there's a sense of belonging
it's your well-being
No it's a quadriginoctuple frap—48 espresso shots,
mocha drizzle, caramel drizzle, white mocha,
hazel nut & coconut milk

so it's best to avoid it all
even the small modules on the side of the road
they're everywhere, those little invaders
I can't bring myself to drive up
for a translunar injection
& order a venti vanilla bean frap with 3 scoops of extra vanilla bean
one scoop of java chips
one pump mocha
one pump peppermint with
half whole milk, half heavy whipping cream—blended—
extra whipped cream & mocha drizzle in the cup on
whipped cream
nope   not even for mission command
not even for all mankind

UNFLINCHING

Under the bed, my anxiety lives, rolling in dust,
and above, my covers are smoothed, my pillow is fluffed.
The old, rusted bed frame cuts tender skin,
and beneath it, in the darkest corners,
a stack of journals are written, yet unread.

On the bed above, covers are smoothed
and my pillow is fluffed,
but I fear the yank of hair and rasp of throat,
because beneath, in the darkest corners,
lurks a stack of journals, all written in,
yet unread.
Through my younger eyes, unblinking in the dark,
words see all, know all.

I fear the yank of hair and rasp of throat,
and the claws that tap and scrape up all my mistakes,
and how my unblinking eyes in the dark,
see all and know all
and greet the days with clenching teeth.

-
The claws tapping and scraping up all my mistakes,
are only words scratching me like an old,
rusted bed frame, cutting my tender skin.
Reading my journals urges me to greet the day
with the power of my clenched teeth—
while under the bed, my anxiety lives,
rolling around in the dust.

POST CARDS TO ALL THE EYES HAVE IT

Maybe, Dear Friend, you're like me and we both have a memory of binocular vision because we can see fine details from afar. Acute color vision colors our ability to go to the Post Office, and stumble and fumble through what kind of stamps and envelopes we need. Imagine our surprise when we googled and found a forum where there are others like us, admitting a fear of being seen. Folx who imagine the perils of making mistakes. We're a sensitive bunch. All our lives we've been called *shy*. There are others like us, who can see prey from a mile away and sense minute movements. Our photoreceptorness is a wide field of view. Together, some of us noted our fears of banks and cash machines and pumping gas. Did you, too, Dear Friend, want to move to Oregon because the law said you couldn't pump your own gas. We could dream, couldn't we. You and I could never live in Europe with all that CCTV. And of course, we're fooling ourselves thinking we'd even navigate an airport with all those rules. We're likely lost before we get lost.

As far as a meet-up, Dear Friend, if we're ever in the same place we'll find each other at the back of the room, having arrived early to sit in the very back near the door. We won't be chatting because that's too forward. But we'll know we're not alone and that's something. Really, *it's everything*. Yet, it's not. We should have a button to wear on our hats or lapels or wear a rubber bracelet. At any event, if we even go anywhere at all, we'll be looking down, pretending to read something. Anything. Don't we think it makes us look smart? We won't sense each other's trembles, hear the heart thumps, note the bump in our throats, or sense when we're holding our breaths, smothering ourselves. But we'll catch each other if we pass out, right? If we get uncomfortable, we'll follow each other out the door when we're pretending not to run.

Outside, we can share cigarettes if we smoke. If we don't, we can sit on a cement bench and watch the frog hopping alone in the grass, see the red fox slink over the hill, and note, without speaking, how the polar bear, and the badger, too, are keeping to themselves.

STAY UP

RAIF JOHNSON-KENNEDY

ABOUT THE POET: RAIF JOHNSON-KENNEDY

RAIF JOHNSON-KENNEDY WAS BORN and raised in Fairbanks Alaska and has been performing poems there since 2004. The release given by the Poetry Slam format as an opportunity to say his thoughts was a life saver for someone who was about to pop. He has both hosted and participated in many Poetry Slams over the years, and although raising a family has taken priority in recent times, he hopes to be involved in many future poetry events so that others may also be able to release and stay inspired.

SYNOPISIS
STAY UP

These poems I hope bring encouragement. There are many ways to fall off track and it is important that as many people as possible stay on their path. I hope these words help do that.

WOLVERINE

You never know how hard you're going to have it
You made it harder when you're trapped within that
last hit
Now you can't stop it
Lord I can't stand it
Watching my kin fall into the cracks around the planet

Goddamn I thought you had it but deep inside that
inner magic
is a lantern and the fact is that the dragons have
engulfed it whole
How many of those that have found their inner glow
Know how to bestow that knowledge on a lost soul

Out of control, eject, or free fall in the tailspin
Goose's ghost is screaming you should never leave your
wingman
So, where you is then
You still have your wings man
Although it's damn impossible when you're swimming
in the quicksand
It'd take a big stand
It'd take a solid plan
It'd take a rehab with a lot of help from the fam
But every time I try and give you a hand
I pull away before we get you on land

It's, "The Killing Joke" gets told with remorse
Afraid I'll get a call to come and ID your corpse
Praying for the day that you can get back on course
And feel breath from the source of the force

I wrote it once that the reason I rapped was to make you
proud
from your side of the tracks
I realize we all can't walk the same path
You had a lot harder we already know that

The wolverine that we saw in the pass
We should have chased it
You heal fast.

BLACK HOLE

The black hole of tragedy
Surrounded by love to quench the gravity
Until all lies even across the plain
Stagnant acidic and basic and same
Mixtures no longer move, ooze into
 an orifice, lock in place
        Orison
Please give me strength

ALADDIN

The ultimate power
 is to be content
And then aid others
 to an extent
All lights are conditional
There is the rub
 and I wish it weren't so
Glow

RIDE OR DIE

Easy dopamine
eventually betrays you
Turn you into nothing
you're supposed to be Atreyu
A never ending story
another hero's journey
Sometimes you are the villain
Sometimes you are the glory
Incorporate your shadow
step into the battle
Help others in the saddle
Until your breath rattles

NOSFERATU

I was right there watching you fall
Made no attempt at a rescue at all
Maybe the way we were meant to evolve
Slip into death and another dissolve

I'm calling it off
My loved one is lost
Thought I'd be the one that've fought
to the end but I can't
Slip through the cracks in the sand
Ash and my man
Dude in the dust
How come my hands couldn't help you get up
 get up, come on you got to, Nosferatu

Oh, the escape is a blessed embrace
Holding you close and engulf like a snake
Make any move on the earth that you choose
Just don't get consumed by the Nosferatu

Exhumin' the human the first steps congruent
to facing the music and making a movement
Illuminate paths on the world like a map
Spirit signs guide you to get back on track

Flowery prose on a white privileged scroll
I've never known diablo obstacles
Trauma induced is the reason assumed
Turning the love into Nosferatu

Writing this now and I don't give a fuck
if you ever get up

if you ever get up
Man, I got my own way that I gotta maintain
Even though all of us all on the plain
and the chain that connects
Everything pulled in vain in a half assed attempt
to get you out of the flame
Get you out of the rain
Off the fast lane
Safe from the pain
get you safe from the pain
Hourglass sand where every damn grain is the time
running out
That is screaming your name
come on you got to

Either ground or the cloud
we end up in the round and the pound
of the heart isn't loud I have found for the saken
have taken a way that will break them
Fast lane to disaster insane zombie cranium
Slow down, turn around please come back you can't
make them,
decisions dissolve cast away in the lake and the brain
and the ripple,
the wave and the simple,
the peace you see there by the shore by the hill now

Deep breath of clean air from the boat you can feel now
The love that there was along the long tundra field now
And floating across in a canoe we can do it
That eagle that nest in that tree now we knew it
And getting too close now we see mother's movement
She swooped down on us as a warning don't do it
don't do it don't do it
Please turn back around
The wind picking up and the waves crashing down

And we paddle and paddle against all the current
When suddenly time to play tag you say "you're it"
Then off to the races across all the playthings
Jump from swings to the slides off the bridges to safety
The ground is all lava, can't touch or you'll lose
"You're cheating"
"No, it isn't, I found special shoes."

CYLINDERS

Broke a four-day fast on bone marrow once
 Odin would be proud
Haven't in over a month
 Current amps around
Are tears supposed to short circuit us
 Draining brain beams down
Fully filling all the lungs
 Extending through the crown

From a pawn to a king with still only one move, up
Lucky on this circle on all cylinders, yup

FIRE

Work harder on the weekend than the week while at
work
Where your passion lies you'll find your purpose and
worth
I was told, do what you love more than you love to do it
But within freedom and discipline an uneven solution
For me at least it seems I keep most dreams incomplete
Failed missions indecisions motivations deplete
The goals you hold will get old and stagnant, it's tragic
You gotta make a move
 Take one step
  Get your candle lit
   Handle it

EMBERS

If those that can fly
 leave others behind
They'll get pulled from the sky
 because everything's tied
together

If those upon high
 let the low die
Is all they'd known gone forever

Inside the ruin
 seeds still an ember
The truth's not all human
 remember

CHOOSE YOUR OWN ADVENTURE

They want your thoughts on the plots
turn it off
and then it stops
Until it's at your doorstep
Still own a door
You ain't poor yet
Torture horror and there's more yet
Make shore sure you're your ore oar for the torrent

Get your shit together
No more posts and no more letters
Inept nomads in the weather
Try and tether on another ember when there's extra

Can't even pull my man out of meth
More like my brother
More like from death
Falling out like all the rest
I must confess I could have tried less

A keeper of brothers without fathers or mothers
Countless haunted encounters
or born under a stubborn star

From the dawn of man to the risk of spam
These lifespans have been survival
"Can't make it alone."
"I know."

ORIGINS

We're a reaction
Within a warm cool spectrum
Hell, call it heaven

When all things join as one
the harmonic occurs
and explodes
oh lord
you can't stop it
That's just a little bit of babble bout the big bang

There's iron in blood
Rivers of stars move through you
Why are we magnets?

AFTERWORD

Shoutout to contributors of the inaugural edition of 100 Fresh Alaskan Poems: Alexis Garcia, Rebecca Goodrich, Kersten Christianson, Ridley Jolena, "PRNsis" Bayinna Ballard, Julie Whatmough, Eric Gordon Johnson, Zoe Woods, Vivian Faith Prescott, and Raif Johnson-Kennedy. Thank you all for trusting me with your words... your poetry, and for extending me a great deal of patience throughout this publishing process. Special thanks to Juanita Magnetek, my lovely wife, for your support, editorial assistance, and for designing our wonderful cover art.

To the readers, I hope this was good for you, as it was for me, to conceive and give birth to this idea of bringing the Edutainment Nite $100 Cash Prize Poetry Slam from stage to page. A question that began to take shape during the pandemic, when I sought ways to continue my small-scale philanthropic efforts of offering $100 to the winner of the monthly poetry slam at the Writer's Block Bookstore & Cafe between 2019 and 2023. At the time, it was the longest, best-attended, and most recognized poetry event in Alaska, a platform that gave space to the state's best and brightest poets. A rarity in itself for a poetry scene to last that long. However, the 2020 pandemic attempted to quell the fire and excitement surrounding the poetry slam, as we continued it virtually.

Recognizing that the poetry slam was in peril without an in-person event to bring community and poets together, I began exploring other avenues to keep its spirit alive. On a personal note, I began my anthropological doctoral studies in 2023, which removed me from being the host of the poetry slam, and as time moved on, the Writer's Block Bookstore & Cafe moved on from being the venue home of the $100 Cash Prize Poetry Slam, essentially fortifying the notion to move the slam from stage to page. With that in mind, with the $100 monthly offering reserved for the poetry slam, Edutainment Nite Publishing chose to give ten poets a $100 stipend for ten thematic poems to compose a one-hundred-poem poetry anthology.

Thus, the success of this work resides in its commitment to community and in continuing to create space... a safe place and platform for first-time poets, emerging poets, marginalized poets, and poets with ties to Alaska. The vision involves publishing a poetry anthology every other year to uplift the aforementioned poets and expand the Alaskan literary landscape to be more inclusive of a wider range of fresh voices.

Thank you for purchasing, reading, and sharing the good news! The Edutainment Nite $100 Cash Prize Poetry Slam lives on in 100 Fresh Alaskan Poems 2026 and beyond—celebrating voices and poetry that inspire our community.

-M.C. MoHagani Magnetek